The Amazing Octopus

Written by Vicki León

Contents

PEARSON

The Octopus

Deep in the ocean lives a creature known for its tricks. It can get out of the tightest places. It can change its shape and its color in less than a second. This creature is **coldblooded** and is called an octopus. More than 150 kinds of octopuses can be found around the world. The smallest is the size of a thumb. The biggest is more than 20 feet from arm tip to arm tip.

An octopus has no **backbone**. It has a body shaped like a balloon that is covered by a **mantle**. It has eight arms. Each arm has rows of **suckers**. Most kinds of octopuses have about 2,000 suckers. These suckers help an octopus to pick up and eat food. They also help it to cling to a hiding place. Octopus arms are always busy. They use their arms to walk, crawl, dig, and eat.

An octopus has two eyes. It can turn its eyes in half circles without moving its head. Its eyesight is very sharp. An octopus uses **gills** and a **funnel** for breathing. Its funnel also helps the octopus move through water. *

Parts of an Octopus

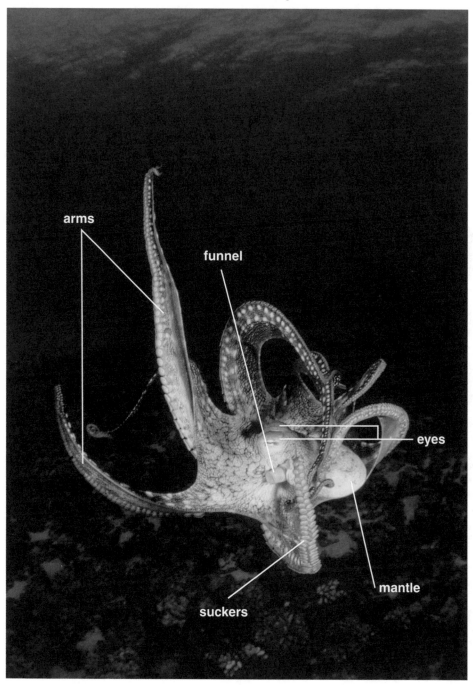

arms

funnel

eyes

mantle

suckers

Amazing Abilities

An octopus eats meat, sees well in the dark, and hunts alone. Each night, the octopus glides along the ocean floor. It uses taste buds along its arms to taste what it touches. That's how it finds and captures food such as crabs, shrimp, and clams. By day, the octopus hunts by spreading its arms and body to create a web. When a meal comes along, the octopus floats down like an open flower and traps it. Most kinds of octopuses shoot poison into their prey. The prey dies quickly.

The octopus tastes everything it touches on the ocean floor.

When alarmed, an octopus can change color.

The octopus uses its skin for different purposes. There are millions of color cells in its skin. When the octopus gets alarmed, the cells get bigger and change color. They can turn red, white, or even two colors at once. Some cells turn shiny colors, such as shades of blue, green, and yellow. A few can become as clear as glass!

Most octopuses are small and shy. They like to hide—or blend in. Besides changing skin color, they can make their skin bumpy or smooth to match where they are. In seconds, the octopus can look like a rock, a plant, or a patch of sand.

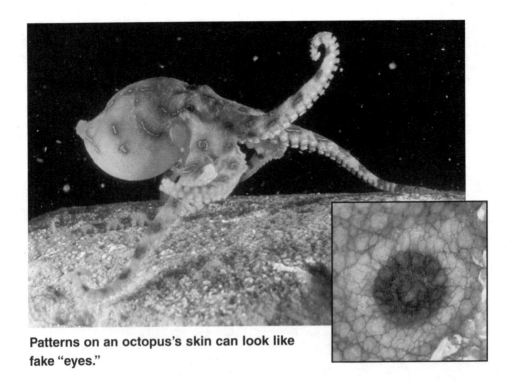

Patterns on an octopus's skin can look like fake "eyes."

The octopus uses tricks to survive. To scare predators, the octopus sometimes puffs up and flashes fake "eyes." These "eyes" are patterns on its skin. An octopus can also shoot a big cloud of ink into the water when frightened. This gives it time to dart away. If an octopus can't get away from a seal or an **eel**, it leaves an arm behind. A new one grows back over time!

Where Octopuses Live

An octopus likes to make its **den** in a cave. Sometimes when a cave is hard to find, an octopus will hunt and kill a large clam. Then it will move into its shell. An octopus has no bones, so it can change into many shapes. It doesn't need much room. A small shell or bottle will do.

Octopuses don't share dens. Once an octopus finds a den, it hides all openings. But at times it tosses scraps from meals out the door. Often these clues attract a moray eel. Then the octopus becomes the eel's dinner.

A frightened octopus shoots a big cloud of ink into the water.

Life Cycle

Octopuses live alone most of their lives. Males and females mate for a short time. Scientists now believe that most males die soon after mating. The female makes a nesting den. She lays up to 100,000 eggs and hangs them from the ceiling of her den. The eggs are about the size and color of **rice grains**.

A female octopus lays up to 100,000 eggs and hangs them from the ceiling of her den.

For up to six months, the female guards the den and cleans the eggs with her suckers. Most females do not eat during this time. When her babies hatch, she aims her funnel like a hose and shoots them out of the den. Then the female dies.

An octopus hatches from an egg.

Only a few babies get past the predators outside the den. Most don't make it. Those that live begin to hunt prey even tinier than they are. Within weeks, the babies double in size. The young octopuses soon mature. Then they look for mates, and the **life cycle** begins once more.

Learning From Octopuses

For years, people have caught octopuses for food. They are a good source of protein. At the same time, humans have feared the octopus. Scary movies and tall tales have made them seem like "sea monsters." Most octopuses are harmless. Some do bite, but only the blue-ringed octopus has enough poison to kill a person.

Scientists are amazed to find what octopuses can do. Some octopuses can "pour" themselves through a tiny hole in a jar lid. Some scientists believe that octopuses can copy each other. They watch and learn how to do tasks. In one study, an octopus learned over time how to open a jar. A second octopus learned the same task quickly—by watching the first one. Their ability to learn makes them quick at solving problems.

An octopus "pours" itself through a tiny hole in a jar.